TABLE OF CONTENTS

I0427915

INTRODUCTION

HANNAH'S STORY

"'If it doesn't work out, I'll just come back with you,' I had told my parents before leaving, secretly hoping I wouldn't have to, but prepared to nevertheless. Having cerebral palsy since birth, I understood well the intricacies involved in ensuring my basic needs—such as getting up, dressing, and going to the restroom—were met. I need assistance with all these tasks. And while I am not able to transfer myself, I'm fairly independent once in my chair.

Although my mom had agreed to stay with me a few days longer to help settle things, I knew there was a possibility I'd have to spend my summer at home in Chicago rather than in the Washington, DC area, where I had accepted an internship with the federal government.

I had a place to stay, a job, and one personal assistant. Despite a variety of unresolved issues I faced, including finding additional personal assistants, my parents had agreed to drive out East. 'If nothing else,' I had jokingly explained, 'consider it a vacation.' The months leading up to coming to the Washington, DC area had been riddled with 'hurdles.' Amazingly, every one of the obstacles had been removed—albeit sometimes at the last minute. From misplaced paperwork to a housing mix-up and no assistants (until days before leaving Chicago), the preparation period had definitely been a character-building and faith-building experience. Through it all, friends encouraged and assured me I'd have plenty to share when everything was said and done. They were right."

Transitioning into adulthood can be awkward for nearly every young person. Some youth with disabilities may need extra supports throughout their transition period in order to make informed choices and become self-sufficient adults. For transition-age youth who use personal assistance services (PAS), issues surrounding managing PAS can be intensified by normal developmental concerns such as striking out on your own, refining your self-identity, and navigating the road into adulthood. Having someone assist you in doing anything—whether it's help with homework, learning to drive, getting dressed, or bathing—is highly personalized. How you approach the tasks associated with your personal care can depend on so many things: your existing knowledge base, willingness to learn and try new things, daily mood, sense of safety, personal preferences, likes, dislikes, specific relationships with your family members and friends, the ability to trust others, and many other intangible factors.

In addition, many systemic barriers complicate the world of PAS. From funding and program eligibility complexities to legal and program culture issues, this mix of personal and systemic challenges can be daunting. This toolkit is meant to help transition-age youth with significant disabilities as well as their family and friends navigate the complex world of PAS. Whether moving from school or a home setting to work, college, or living on their own, transition-age youth and their families or friends would benefit from preparing for and taking care of these issues.

This toolkit is meant to be practical. Users are strongly encouraged to adapt the examples to their own situations, and to pick and choose the strategies that work best for them. It's not necessary to use the entire toolkit, nor is it essential to use the tools in order. It is also not intended to serve as a legal reference. Please consult other resources for this information.

THE BASICS OF PAS

DIFFERING DEFINITIONS

Before getting into too much depth regarding finding and managing your own PAS, it's important to have a basic understanding of the varying definitions of PAS, knowledge of commonly used terms, and a grasp of the common legal issues that arise surrounding the issue of PAS.

The term "**personal assistance services**" has become the more preferred term in the disability community to refer to someone, or several people, who assist a person with a disability in performing certain tasks during the course of the day that s/he cannot perform on his/her own. Other terms are still used, such as personal assistant (PA), Personal Care Assistant (PCA), or Attendant. While it may seem confusing, it is important to understand the use and meaning of the term PAS as there are subtle differences in various programs and settings that can affect eligibility for programs, funding, and specific services.

The World Institute on Disability defines PAS as "assistance, under maximum feasible user control, with tasks that maintain well-being, comfort, safety, personal appearance, and interactions within the community and society as a whole" (Holt, Chambless & Hammond, 2006). In general, PAS is used by persons with disabilities to perform tasks that the person would perform for him/herself if s/he did not have a disability. It can include tasks that range from reading, communication, and performing manual tasks (e.g., turning pages) to bathing, eating, toileting, personal hygiene, and dressing (Silverstein, 2003).

Another way to think about PAS, especially for Medicaid program eligibility purposes, is as a "range of human assistance provided to persons with disabilities and chronic conditions of all ages, which enables them to accomplish tasks they would normally do for themselves if they did not have a disability." Assistance may be hands-on (actually performing a task for an individual) or cueing so that the person performs the task by him/herself. Such assistance most often relates to performance of activities of daily living

(ADLs) and instrumental activities of daily living (IADLs) (State Medicaid Manual, Section 4460).

And to push the definition even further, the Rehabilitation Act and the Ticket to Work and Work Incentives Improvement Act define PAS as "a range of services provided by one or more persons designed to assist an individual with a disability to perform daily living activities on or off the job that the individual would typically perform if the individual did not have a disability. Such services shall be designed to increase the individual's control in life and ability to perform everyday activities on or off the job" (Ticket to Work and Work Incentives Improvement Act, 42 USC 1320b-22(b)(2)(B)(ii); 34 CFR 361.5(39) and the Rehabilitation Act, 34 CFR 361.5(39)).

However, over the last several years, legislation floating (and dying) in Congress designed to create a comprehensive national PAS system has consistently used the following more specific definition of PAS: "…tasks include: 1) personal maintenance and hygiene activities such as dressing, grooming, feeding, bathing, respiration, and toilet functions, including bowel, bladder, catheter and menstrual tasks; 2) mobility tasks such as getting into and out of bed, wheelchair, or tub; 3) household maintenance tasks such as cleaning, shopping, meal preparation laundering, and long-term heavy cleaning and repairs; 4) infant and child-related tasks such as bathing, diapering, and feeding; 5) cognitive or life management activities such as money management, planning, and decision making; 6) security-related services such as interpreting for people with hearing or speech difficulties and reading for people with visual disabilities" (Glazier, 2001).

UNDERSTANDING KEY TERMS

In the realm of PAS, certain terms are critical to understand in order to protect your civil rights. Here are some key terms you need to know:

- **Activities of Daily Living:** These are things you do every day such as dressing, grooming, bathing, eating, positioning, transferring, and toileting.

- **Health-Related Functions:** Services that must be delegated or assigned by a licensed health care professional, such as a nurse or doctor. Health-related functions are usually required to be provided under the direction of a qualified professional (QP) or a doctor. Examples of health-related functions are special skin care, non-sterile catheter care, tube feedings, and respiratory assistance.

- **Home Health Agency:** Home health agencies usually have a license from the Department of Health or other disability-related department and are Medicare certified. These agencies typically provide skilled nursing visits, home health aide visits, occupational and physical therapy (OT/PT) visits, as well as PAS.

- **Instrumental Activities of Daily Living:** These activities include personal hygiene, light housework, laundry, meal preparation, transportation, grocery shopping, using the telephone, medication management, and money management.

- **Major Bodily Functions:** These include but are not limited to the operation of a major bodily function, including but not limited to, functions of immune system, normal cell growth, digestive, bowel, bladder, neurological, brain, respiratory, circulatory, endocrine, and reproductive functions.

- **Major Life Activities:** Caring for oneself, performing mental tasks, seeing, hearing, eating, sleeping, walking, standing, lifting, bending, speaking, breathing, learning, reading, concentrating, thinking, communicating, and working.

- **Personal Care Provider Organizations:** Sometimes called "PCA Agencies." These are community-based organizations or agencies that only provide PAS.

- **Reasonable Accommodation:** A modification or adjustment to a job that enables a qualified individual with a disability to perform the job functions and thus enjoy equal employment benefits and privileges.

- **Workplace Personal Assistance Services:** Workplace PAS comprises task-related assistance at work, including readers, interpreters, and help with lifting or reaching. Non-essential tasks may also be re-assigned to co-workers. Workplace PAS might include personal care-related assistance such as helping someone with eating, drinking, or using the restroom while at the job site (Krause, 2007).

DISTINGUISHING BETWEEN JOB-RELATED AND PERSONAL PAS

The Americans with Disabilities Act (ADA) of 1990 is a civil rights law that bans discrimination on the basis of disability. Under the ADA, an employer with 15 or more employees must make reasonable accommodation for an otherwise qualified applicant or employee unless the employer can demonstrate the accommodation would impose an undue hardship on the operation of the business (29 CFR 1630.9(a)). A qualified person with a disability must meet the skill, experience, education, and other job-related requirements (of a position held or desired) and—with or without reasonable accommodation—be able to perform the essential functions of a job (29 CFR 1630.2(m)).

Thus, the ADA requires employers to provide PAS to an applicant or employee with a disability so long as the services are job related and not primarily for personal benefit. Job related assistance in the performance of such tasks as reading, communication, the performance of nonessential manual tasks, and business-related travel may be considered reasonable accommodations. Assistance with tasks such as eating, toileting, dressing, and personal hygiene are primarily personal in nature and generally are not considered reasonable accommodations (Silverstein, 2003, p. 2). Assistive technologies such as closed caption television, text messaging, screen magnification, and reaching devices complement work-related PAS. However, assistive technologies are not workplace PAS (DOL/ODEP (2006), p. 3).

These lines can become very blurry, especially if an employer provides personal care as a part of workplace PAS. It is important to know the rules and the legal interpretations. Since the provision of some PAS is at the discretion of the employer, it is always a good idea to communicate directly with your supervisor about specific PAS workplace needs.

According to the Equal Employment Opportunity Commission (EEOC), reasonable accommodation under the ADA can include providing work-related personal assistance to help an employee with a disability perform marginal job functions. The EEOC includes the following example in its ADA Technical Assistance Manual: "Some other accommodations that may be appropriate include . . . providing a personal assistant for certain job-related functions, such as a page turner for a person who has no hands, or a travel assistant to act as a sighted guide to assist a blind employee on an occasional business trip" (EEOC, 1992).

Use of the term PAS to describe readers and interpreters and people helping to carry out tasks at work is often confusing, because PAS is so commonly thought to be mostly about someone helping provide personal care (Stoddard & Kraus, 2006). It is important for employees with disabilities to understand what workplace PAS (WPAS) is and is not. A workplace personal assistant does not perform the job duties or take care of daily personal needs. The employer is not responsible for providing this type of service.

A workplace personal assistant only provides assistance with the actual job tasks in order to increase the efficiency and productivity of an employee with a disability (Turner, 2007).

The distinction is mainly driven by this factor: who is responsible for providing and funding WPAS. While the employer most often covers task-related WPAS, personal care-related tasks are left to the employee. Business travel is a commonly highlighted exception. When an employee requiring WPAS needs to travel for work, the employer may need to consider providing assistance both for personal care-related tasks and WPAS for the employee during travel.

The EEOC clarifies that employers are not required to pay for or arrange personal care-related assistance in the workplace, since such accommodations are related to meeting an individual's personal needs. Employers must, however, consider both allowing employees with disabilities to bring their personal assistants into the workplace and providing space for ensuring the employee's personal needs (i.e., eating, drinking, toileting, etc.) are met.

The EEOC also notes that employers may choose to go beyond the requirements of the ADA when providing job assistants. For example, "supported employment" programs may provide free job coaches and other assistance to enable individuals with significant disabilities to learn and/or to progress in jobs. These programs typically require a range of modifications and adjustments to customary employment practices. Some of these modifications may also be required by the ADA as reasonable accommodations (EEOC, 1992).

CLAIRE'S STORY

As she approached high school graduation, Claire began looking at different colleges. "I was pushing away from having my parents as my main caregivers," she says. "It was kind of a scary thing, but I wanted to be out on my own."

Perhaps you've reached a place in life when you're ready to be more independent and even live on your own. Some of us are fortunate enough to have friends or relatives around the same age who have been through the process before: they're living on their own, paying their rent, managing their bills, and maintaining their own place.

If so, begin by asking them what it takes to be more independent. Chances are that the positive experiences, such as meeting new people, having more freedom, and learning new things, have been balanced with a number of challenges (i.e., bad roommate situations, conflicts with apartment managers, and the difficulty of learning to manage a household). Nevertheless, don't let these realities deter you from pursuing and achieving your goal of independence. Making any sort of life change has both its drawbacks and benefits.

It's important to make an informed decision. This requires some serious needs assessment, targeted research, and personal and financial planning for anyone. You may face the additional consideration of needing to find your own PAS.

In addition to talking to both friends and family, take some time to assess your own needs. Be honest and realistic with yourself, and consider the type of living situation that suits you best: living on your own or with roommates. Think about how you will pay for food, utilities, and other essentials. Take into account your transportation needs as well as your personal assistance requirements. It may be helpful to involve your friends and family in the evaluation process to ensure you consider a variety of perspectives.

JEFF'S STORY

"We have had to 'wing it' as Jeff moved from childhood to adolescence to young adulthood," Jeff's mom, Raechelle, confides. "At each stage, Jeff had different needs," she says. "Right now we are trying to figure out how to pass the torch of responsibility (for PAS) to Jeff." Raechelle and her husband are concerned about what will happen to Jeff when they are no longer available to help him choose and direct personal assistants. They want him to be as independent as possible but lack guidance on how to make that happen.

Drafting a list of key considerations/issues to address will help you gain a better understanding of the areas that need some attention if you are to live on your own and take charge of your own PAS. They may include the following:

Your personal care needs (i.e., dressing, grooming, personal care and hygiene, housekeeping, meal preparation, transportation, companionship, medical issues, etc.);

When you will need assistance and for how long: this would include the amount of time you will need assistance each day and during which periods of the day (i.e., morning, evening, 24 hours, etc.);

Personal assistant preferences: what characteristics might an assistant have that will make you most comfortable (i.e., gender, age, ethnicity, disability, language, reading and communication skills, citizenship status, personal hygiene, patience, compassion, strength, ability to listen, talkative, nonsmoker, etc.); and,

Knowledge, skills, and abilities to address difficult issues with your personal assistant(s) (i.e., money management, time management, conflict, romance, sexuality, etc.).

Taking some time to consider your personal preferences and needs in the beginning will go a long way in helping you effectively recruit, interview, hire, and manage your personal assistant services in the future. On the pages that follow are some checklists and tools meant to help guide you in thinking through these important topics. Keep in mind that these are only examples, and that many community programs that assist people with disabilities (such as independent living centers and community rehabilitation programs) also may have helpful planning tools and tips. The *Additional Resources* section at the end of the toolkit provides links to locate such community-based organizations.

CLAIRE'S STORY

Claire currently has a roommate who helps with a variety of tasks. "I have a roommate who is more like a friend although she does some of my personal care," says Claire. "Sometimes she cooks meals for dinner, but not always." The amount of time her roommate assists her varies at times. Occasionally, she assists Claire in the restroom. "I find that if I drink coffee or alcohol I need to go to the bathroom more," Claire offers, "so I have to limit my drinking."

THINKING OUTSIDE THE BOX: SERVICE DOGS

The tools to help people with disabilities live independently don't just come in the form of other people or services. Over the last 20 years, a growing number of people with disabilities have come to rely on animals, such as dogs, monkeys, and ponies, for assistance. Since space is limited, the discussion here will focus on dogs. But before considering whether a dog might help you be more independent, it's important to make the distinction between assistance dogs and service dogs.

Service Dog: A dog that works for individuals with disabilities other than blindness or deafness. They are trained to perform a wide variety of tasks including but not limited to: pulling a wheelchair, bracing, retrieving, alerting to a medical crisis, and providing assistance in a medical crisis (Assistance Dogs International, 2009).

Assistance Dog: A generic term for a guide, hearing, or service dog specifically trained to do more than one task to

mitigate the effects of an individual's disability. The presence of a dog for protection, personal defense, or comfort does not qualify that dog as an assistance dog (Assistance Dogs International, 2009).

Maybe the idea of having a dog help you pick up things or pull off your socks appeals to you. If you're an animal lover, the thought of being able to take a dog nearly everywhere might seem too good to be true. But, there is a difference between the idea of a service dog and the actual responsibility of a live animal. Service dogs are specially trained, but they are still dogs. They are not machines, and they cannot be put on the shelf. Responsible dog ownership takes time and energy. A service dog increases independence, but also requires sacrifices and adjustments.

While it is perfectly okay to have assistance in caring for a service dog, the human partner should take an active and primary role in making sure the dog's needs are met. For the bonding of a team to take place, the human partner needs to be the most important person in the dog's life. This means making time to exercise, groom, and even play with the dog. It's important to take an active role in the day-to-day activities, so when you're alone the dog will recognize your leadership and respond.

Being Realistic in Your Expectations
If you are exploring getting a service dog, there are some questions you need to be able to answer for yourself.

Would you consider yourself a "dog person"?

It's highly likely that a service dog would spend more time with you than any personal assistant or family member.

Given the dog's responsibilities, this means the dog will likely sleep next to you, pick up things with its mouth, and need to be walked regularly. It also means that your clothes and your living space will regularly be covered in dog hair. So, if dog slobber and animal fur are anywhere on your list of pet peeves, you may want to rethink the idea of getting a service dog.

What types of things would a service dog do for you?

Make sure that your expectations are realistic. For example, perhaps you're considering having a service dog to help you get around campus in your manual wheelchair. It's important to know these dogs cannot pull a wheelchair entirely on their own. In order for the dog to perform the skill, the individual must be able to move the chair somewhat.

While the general public may consider getting a dog for protection, keep in mind service dogs are not trained to be protective. In addition, while many organizations teach service dogs basic and specialized commands, working effectively as a team requires hours of ongoing training that help the dog learn new skills and review those previously learned.

Do you have the financial resources to provide for basic needs of the dog (i.e., food, veterinary bills, and grooming costs)?

Many organizations that train service dogs will extensively screen applicants to ensure they have the need for a dog, the resources to care for the animal, and the time necessary to maintain the animal's skills and well-being. These organizations often recognize that individuals with disabilities may receive financial assistance from other sources. This factor alone will not preclude an individual from being eligible for a service dog. Whether you receive assistance or not, it's important to seriously consider the cost involved in caring for an animal.

Do you have someone who could serve as a training assistant?

Some agencies require that you bring a training assistant with you when you get the dog. If not, it's still important to consider having someone who could help if you run into problems teaching the dog new skills and strengthening existing commands. The organization may provide support to recipients, but sometimes an informal assistant can also be helpful—especially if you find that you need basic assistance on a regular basis.

Are you prepared to be completely responsible for the life, health, safety, care, and needs of a living being?

This animal will be your responsibility 24 hours a day, 7 days a week, 365 days a year.

Choosing a Program

Not all assistance dog programs are created equally. Programs vary widely in terms of training philosophies, structure of the training process, the source of potential service dogs, and cost for potential recipients. It's in your best interest to do as much research as possible to see what works best for you and your situation. The first step to getting a service dog is finding a reputable program with skilled trainers and a proven track record. Programs vary in terms of their structure and cost to recipients. Potential recipients typically must complete an application and screening process before being placed on a waiting list for a service dog. The waiting time for a service dog can be as long as two to four years, depending on the organization, their training methods, and the types of dogs selected for training.

If the dog is trained through a specific program or organization, it is likely that some basic training will occur before you train with the dog. Depending on the structure of the program, basic training can last anywhere from six months to a year and a half. Following basic training, recipients are usually invited to a training class—usually several weeks in length—to learn the commands and handling skills needed for working with a service dog.

Shelter Dogs Versus Specially-Bred Dogs

Some people believe it's more beneficial to train dogs selected from the local shelters. Although there are practices in place for evaluating these animals' potential for service work, it is impossible to know for certain whether something in the animal's background may lead to irrational or inappropriate behavior later (i.e., biting someone who approaches them too quickly or being overly frightened by noises or activity such as a car backfiring).

HANNAH'S STORY

"Upon leaving team training, I had my serious doubts as to whether I had made the right decision. I had even talked with the trainers about not taking Max home, because he wasn't responding as I thought he should. The trainers reassured me Max knew the commands and would perform them well. I just needed to relax and give him time. Sounds easy enough, right??? Maybe for someone who is not a perfectionist, but I wanted Max to do things well, and do them right the first time, without having to repeat commands. What I had to realize was that Max was not a robot. Our relationship depended on more than just what Max could do for me. It really depended on really loving one another. The trainer's homework assignment for me as I left training was to go have fun with your dog. For someone who likes cut and dry instructions, this seemed crazy. But I'm here to tell you that it worked. Although my high expectations for Max have not changed, I have realized that he is not perfect and neither am I."

Programs that breed and train their own dogs spend months, even years, evaluating the animal's temperament, physical health, and overall work ethic. Oftentimes, if an animal is not suited for service work, this is determined well before a potential recipient enters the picture. Be wary of an agency that promises too much too soon. Also, take time to ask questions about the program's certification. Assistance Dogs International (ADI) is a nonprofit organization that helps develop standards for various types of working animals, such as therapy dogs, companion animals, guide dogs, and service animals. Organizations and programs accredited by ADI have met certain standards.

According to ADI, the number of shelter dogs that are viable as hearing and service dogs is exaggerated by some organizations. The organization explains that selection of a dog is critical and much more involved than it first may seem.

"A Service Dog candidate should be between 18 months to 2 years old. A younger dog will not show its adult temperament and will not have adult bone structure for hip/shoulder/elbow x-rays. Older than two reduces the amount of time the dog will be able to work....This will eliminate 60 to 80 percent of the dogs in the shelter. Dog size and inappropriate breeds will eliminate another 10 to 20 percent. Temperament tests will eliminate many more. In general, during a visit to the shelter only 1 to 5 percent of the dogs might qualify. Fifty percent of the dogs selected will have...health problems that will then disqualify them" (ADI, 2009).

Considering Costs
Most organizations will charge a minimal fee or no fee at all for the dog, despite the fact that it may cost up to $50,000 to raise and train a prospective service dog. Other organizations and private trainers will expect potential recipients to cover some costs. If you apply to and are accepted by a provider organization that belongs to Assistance Dogs United Campaign, you can apply to receive a voucher that pays the cost of your dog.

While there may be no fee for the dog, you may be required to pay an application fee. In addition, you may be asked to cover your travel and lodging expenses while in training. Some organizations have facilities for potential recipients to stay in, while others may have arrangements with hotels and restaurants in their area. Keep in mind there will also be long-term costs of maintaining your dog's health, such as annual shots, food, and potential grooming costs (e.g., trimming your dog's nails).

ESTABLISHING A PLAN

We all have areas and skills in which we can grow. Think about what you want to learn or need to know before moving out on your own or taking more responsibility for your personal care needs. As the example below illustrates, it may be doing a task around the house. It could also include such goals as developing and maintaining a budget, learning to use public transportation, or strengthening your personal advocacy skills. The following pages provide an example goal and the resources, activities and steps necessary to achieve it, as well as a blank form for you to use in determining your own goals.

Goals for Living Independently (Sample)
Goal #1: Learning how to do laundry

People to Help Me Reach that Goal:

Mom and my friend, Janet

Resources to Help Me Reach that Goal:

The back of the laundry detergent container and the inside lid of the washing machine

Planned Completion Date:

August 2009

Activities to Reaching that Goal:

- Learning to sort clothing and read clothing labels
- Understanding appropriate settings on the washing machine for different types of clothing
- Learning the different settings on the dryer
- Knowing how to iron different types of clothing

Target Dates for Completing Interim Activities:

- Learning to sort clothing and read clothing labels—June 16
- Understanding appropriate settings on the washing machine for different types of clothing – June 30
- Learning different settings on the dryer – July 5
- Knowing how to iron different types of clothing—July 25

Notes on Your Progress:

June 5 – had some trouble sorting laundry and accidentally put a pink shirt with white pants. July 19 – learned today how to iron a button-down shirt.... did most of it myself, with only a little bit of help from my mom.

Goals for Living Independently Worksheet

Goal:

People to Help Me Reach that Goal:

Resources to Help Me Reach that Goal:

Planned Completion Date:

Activities to Reaching that Goal:

Target Dates for Completing Interim Activities:

Notes on Your Progress:

Independent Living Checklist

While moving out on your own can be exciting, it requires a whole new level of responsibility. Being more independent means taking an active role in your health and wellness, personal care, job training, school work, and other areas of your life.

Below are some questions to ask yourself to see whether you are prepared to live more independently. You may not be able to answer "yes" (or "always") to every question listed, but you should be familiar with where to go for assistance.

Overall Independence

Do you have any savings?	☐ Yes	☐ No
Do you have a source of steady income?	☐ Yes	☐ No
Are you contributing to the household income (e.g., paying rent, utilities, etc.)?	☐ Yes	☐ No
Are you able to get from place to place independently?	☐ Yes	☐ No
Do you have a place to live or have you begun looking for one?	☐ Yes	☐ No

Social Supports and Staying Emotionally Healthy

Do you have friends that you spend time with on a regular basis?	☐ Yes	☐ No
Do you regularly communicate with family and friends?	☐ Yes	☐ No
Is there at least one person you talk to when you feel sad, nervous, or things aren't going well?	☐ Yes	☐ No
Are you familiar with the common symptoms of depression?	☐ Yes	☐ No
Do you seek help from others when you experience those symptoms?	☐ Yes	☐ No

What are your hobbies? Or, what do you enjoy doing?

Do you regularly make time for these activities?	☐ Yes	☐ No

Staying Physically Healthy

If you take medications, do you know the name, dosage, reason, and potential side effects for each prescription?	☐ Yes	☐ No
Do you take your medication as prescribed and without being prompted?	☐ Yes	☐ No
Have you taken time to learn about the options available for preventing pregnancy, HIV/AIDS, and sexually transmitted diseases?	☐ Yes	☐ No

Do you independently and effectively handle your personal hygiene? ☐ Yes ☐ No

Are you familiar with the risks associated with smoking, drinking, and using drugs? ☐ Yes ☐ No

Do you exercise regularly? ☐ Yes ☐ No

Are you satisfied with your current weight? ☐ Yes ☐ No

School and Work

What type of things are you good at?

What topics or careers would you like to learn more about? ☐ Yes ☐ No

Do you have career goals? ☐ Yes ☐ No

Are you familiar with the options available to help cover the cost of job training or college? ☐ Yes ☐ No

Do you volunteer regularly? ☐ Yes ☐ No

Do you attend classes/work regularly? ☐ Yes ☐ No

Do you think that your school/work assignments are at the right level for you? ☐ Yes ☐ No

Are you doing well in school and/or at work? ☐ Yes ☐ No

Accessing Health Care

How is your health care paid for?

Who is your family doctor (or, what is the name of the clinic you go to for care)?

Do you regularly schedule and get to medical and dental appointments independently? ☐ Yes ☐ No

Are you independent in your health care decision making? ☐ Yes ☐ No

Are you familiar with how to use your insurance or medical card? ☐ Yes ☐ No

Are your immunizations current? ☐ Yes ☐ No

Have you found an adult health care provider? ☐ Yes ☐ No

Have you had your first appointment with your adult providers? ☐ Yes ☐ No

IDENTIFYING WHAT YOU'RE LOOKING FOR IN A PERSONAL ASSISTANT

Once you've determined that you'll need personal assistants, the next step is to figure out their responsibilities, hours of work, and scheduling. The worksheets in this section are intended to serve in determining what you want and need from your assistants. These sheets may also be helpful in communicating with your assistants once they start working. Since you are now the boss, it's important to establish and maintain good communication with your employees.

Here are a few other things to consider:

- Which tasks will you need help with? Which tasks can you do on your own?

- Approximately how many hours of help will you need? Per day? Per week? [If you don't know, begin to keep track of the general times during the day (and for how long) your friends/family assist you. Under different circumstances, you may require more or less assistance, but keeping track at least provides a starting point.]

- How will you manage/schedule your assistants to ensure that you receive assistance as needed? Will you have your personal assistants come at scheduled times throughout the day and the week? Will you have the personal assistants live with you or will they come in on an as-needed basis? [Each option has advantages and drawbacks associated with it. To help determine the option that works best for you, talk to others who are currently employing personal assistants and consult the Additional Resources section of this manual.]

- How many assistants will you have? Will you have one assistant or multiple assistants? Consider what happens when one person goes out of town or is sick.

Make sure that you are honest with both yourself and with your personal assistant(s) about what's important to you. Because this can be a very personal relationship, it is critical to be upfront about your expectations. Don't consider anything too trivial or too embarrassing to mention.

Each of us has our own habits, likes, and dislikes. Sometimes we do things a certain way simply because we prefer to, and other times there may be a particular reason. For example, if you use a wheelchair you may prefer not to wear your seat belt. Or, when assisting you in dressing it may be easiest for the personal assistant to begin on one side versus another due to your limited range of motion. Many of us may not think too much about our daily routines, oftentimes because they are so familiar. But if you use PAS it's important to consider in detail both the type of help needed from others and the way you like things done. Making a potential personal assistant aware of these preferences and habits can make his/her job much easier and reduce your level of frustration.

Use the following spreadsheet to consider your own activities of daily living, and where you need help from a personal assistant. It may also be useful to make notes on specific ways a potential assistant could best help you. While it is not necessary to share these charts with your employees, you may certainly choose to do so. More than anything, this should be an opportunity to give thoughtful consideration on how to best communicate your needs to a potential personal assistant.

Activities of Daily Living Worksheet

Spreadsheet for Activities of Daily Living

Activity	No Assistance	Partial Assistance	Full Assistance
Mobility—wheelchair (includes pushing a manual wheelchair, clearing a path for the wheelchair, opening doors, daily maintenance of the wheelchair)			
Positioning (includes amount of help needed for comfort or to relieve pressure while sitting or sleeping or positioning of pillows or wedges)			
Toileting (includes assistance needed for bowel programming, catheter and/or colostomy cares, and general toileting assistance)			
Transfers (includes moving from one position to another. Example: moving from bed to a wheelchair or sitting to standing position)			
Medications (includes medications you need to take in the morning, evening, during the day, and/or during sleeping hours)			

Meal Planning and Food Preparation	No Assistance	Partial Assistance	Full Assistance
Menu planning			
Grocery shopping			
Putting food away in cupboards and refrigerator			
Preparing food (cutting, cooking)			
Putting food on plates and table			
Serving food			
Clearing the table			
Putting away leftovers			
Washing dishes/putting dishes in dishwasher			

Laundry	No Assistance	Partial Assistance	Full Assistance
Sorting clothes			
Putting soap in the washing machine			
Putting clothes in the washing machine			
Putting clothes in the dryer			
Folding clothes			
Ironing clothes			
Putting clothes away			

Medical Appointments	No Assistance	Partial Assistance	Full Assistance
Assistance into vehicle			
Accompanying to appointment			
Help into/out of the building and office			
Registering as a patient			
Going into exam room			
Taking notes during exam			
Filling prescriptions			
Transferring onto exam tables/chairs			

Light Housekeeping and Chores	No Assistance	Partial Assistance	Full Assistance
Sweeping			
Mopping			
Vacuuming			
Dusting			
Taking out the garbage			
Making the bed			
Cleaning the windows			
Cleaning the bedroom			
Cleaning the kitchen			
Cleaning the bathroom			

Shopping	No Assistance	Partial Assistance	Full Assistance
Preparing a shopping list			
Assistance into the vehicle/nearest public transportation			
Help into/out of the store			
Taking the items off the shelves			
Carrying the items/pushing the cart			
Handling money			
Loading/unloading purchases into/from vehicle			
Putting items away at home			

Outings/Events	No Assistance	Partial Assistance	Full Assistance
Keeping a calendar of events			
Getting directions			
Assistance into a vehicle			
Help into/out of the building or event			
Help at the event			

Other Activities	No Assistance	Partial Assistance	Full Assistance
Paying bills			
Typing/writing			
Organizing papers			
Getting mail			

DETERMINING YOUR WEEKLY SCHEDULE

As you evaluate the areas and tasks with which you will need assistance, it is useful to consider what a potential schedule might look like. This will be beneficial in recruiting and interviewing potential candidates, who will undoubtedly ask what a typical day might look like for them if they are hired. It will also provide a clearer idea of how much assistance you will need at different times of the day. Finally, developing a weekly schedule can help your assistants learn your routine and ensure that critical activities are completed regularly.

Weekly Schedule (Sample)

Morning Tasks/Cares	

Everyday	Giving morning medications
	Draining leg bag
	Changing catheter and cleaning area
	Grooming
	     – Washing face and upper body
	     – Brushing teeth
	     – Combing hair and/or applying make up
	     – Applying deodorant
	Dressing
	     – Getting clothes out
	     – Putting clothes on
	Transferring to wheelchair
	     – Preparing chair
	Transferring to and positioning in chair
	Preparing breakfast

Morning Tasks/Cares	
Monday – Friday	*In addition to the tasks for every day:* *Showering and washing hair* *Preparing lunch for the next day*

Morning Tasks/Cares	
Saturday – Sunday	*In addition to the tasks listed for every day:* *Preparing lunch*

Evening Tasks/Cares	
Everyday	*Preparing dinner* *Cleaning kitchen* *Giving evening medications* *Helping with undressing* *Transferring to bed and positioning in bed* *Emptying leg bag* *Cleaning urinary bags* *Charging wheelchair*

Evening Tasks/Cares	
Monday – Friday	*In addition to the tasks listed for every day:* *Assisting with suppositories, evacuation, and clean-up*

Evening Tasks/Cares	
Saturday – Sunday	*In addition to the tasks listed for every day:* *Preparing lunch*

Weekly Housekeeping Chores	
Monday	Laundry
Tuesday	Dusting and vacuuming
Wednesday	Grocery shopping
Thursday	Cleaning kitchen and bathroom
Friday	Taking out recycling and garbage

Weekly Schedule Worksheet

Morning Tasks/Cares	
Everyday	

Morning Tasks/Cares	
Monday – Friday	In addition to the tasks listed for every day:

Morning Tasks/Cares	
Saturday – Sunday	In addition to the tasks listed for every day:

Evening Tasks/Cares	
Everyday	

Evening Tasks/Cares	
Tuesday, Thursday, and Saturday	In addition to the tasks listed for every day:

Weekly Housekeeping Chores	
Monday	
Tuesday	
Wednesday	
Thursday	
Friday	

COVERING THE COST OF PAS

Once you know the type of assistance you'll need, it's time to begin thinking about how you will cover the cost of PAS. The options vary from state to state and are sometimes based on the individual's income and the type of assistance needed. The information provided below should serve as a starting point for understanding the overall structure and options available.

> Typically, PAS are paid for in one of three ways: 1) Cash benefits, where payments go to qualified consumers or their representative payees; 2) vendor payments to provider agencies, where a case manager determines the types and amounts of covered services, and arranges for and pays authorized providers to deliver the services; and 3) vouchers where consumers use funds for authorized purchases. For specific information, it is best to talk to someone in your state and/or county.

Below are the major sources of funding for PAS:

■ Private Funds: The most common payment source for personal assistants is the individual and/or family who are receiving the service.

■ Private Health Insurance: This option is typically not well accessed by people with significant disabilities for several reasons. First, private health insurance is most often paid for by employers and provided only to full-time employees. Second, since people with disabilities experience substantially higher rates of unemployment. They often cannot get employer provided health care. Finally, private insurance policies often cover only acute (not chronic) care.

■ Federal/State Funded Programs: There are several programs that can assist with locating and/or paying for

PAS on a limited basis. For example, Vocational Rehabilitation programs, funded through a combination of federal and state dollars, may support PAS if it can be demonstrated that such services are essential to achieving an employment outcome.

Medicaid: Depending on the state, Medicaid might pay for personal care assistants, case management, therapeutic services, medical care, technological and physical aids, and other services. Information on Medicaid options in your state can be found at: http://www.cms.hhs.gov/home/medicaid.asp.

Depending on your financial situation, you will want to learn more about your eligibility for Medicaid. While Medicaid eligibility varies from state to state, generally people with disabilities and other whose income is equal to or less than the federal poverty level are eligible. In addition to income, other factors may "categorically" qualify you for Medicaid benefits.

People with disabilities who receive Supplemental Security Income (SSI) are "categorically" eligible for Medicaid health care benefits. Many states have Medicaid Buy-In programs in which you have to pay a fee to retain your Medicaid health care support while you work. Some states even support workplace PAS when the services are not covered by the employer as a reasonable accommodation. As part of your assessment process, you should look into as many of these programs as possible. More information is available at: http://www.cms.gov/MedicaidEligibility/

"The PAS system is confusing and contradictory. The funding sources are hard to understand and the guidelines are unclear. One thing that Jeff could really use is stability in assistants, but the system makes that difficult to achieve," Raechelle, Jeff's mom, explains. "For example, Jeff is currently covered by the Choice Program for the Aging and Disabled for 19.5 hours a week and the Support System Waiver for nine hours," Raechelle continues, referring to two different state-offered Medicaid-supported options for paying for PAS for people with significant disabilities. "It would be helpful to have the comprehensive waiver," she says, "so that Jeff's needs could be covered by one program with one set of rules, but it is usually such a long wait before that becomes possible."

Social Security Programs: Social Security's Supplemental Support Income (SSI) can play a significant role in helping you live independently and become eligible for Medicaid's health care coverage. There are also a number of "incentives" associated with the Social Security programs to assist in purchasing needed services and supports and saving funds as you move toward self-sufficiency. To find the Social Security office nearest you, visit: https://secure.ssa.gov/apps6z/FOLO/fo001.jsp

Vocational Rehabilitation: The Vocational Rehabilitation program can be instrumental in helping you get job readiness training, cover personal assistance and other services, and secure employment. The following fact sheet and additional links provide more detailed information:
http://www.disabilityrightsca.org/pubs/503401.pdf
http://askjan.org/cgi-win/TypeQuery.exe?902

State Funds for Residential Services: Many states may use their own funding sources to cover the costs of supporting people with disabilities in both their homes and in community residential options (i.e., group homes and apartment programs).

- **Employers:** Work-related PAS may be covered by employers as an accommodation under the ADA (e.g., paying for a personal assistant while traveling for business or to assist in job-related tasks).

SEARCHING FOR PAS

The search for PAS can, at first, seem a bit overwhelming, especially since there is no national database or structure to connect all the different sources of PAS. Talk to anyone who uses PAS, and they will tell you that there are a wide variety of ways to find the assistance you'll need. They will also likely tell you that they've tried almost all the resources described here at one time or another. Unfortunately, there is no one-size-fits-all method. Over time, you will likely have to vary your search methods, since it is unlikely that one method will work every time. Keep in mind that the funding for your personal assistance may impact how you go about finding a personal assistant and whom exactly you hire.

You will want to be familiar with the various sources in your community for locating assistants, such as from PAS registries, independent living centers, community provider agencies, etc. You will need to think carefully about the kinds of things that you need from your personal assistant and what you want the job to entail. You will also need to understand the going wage in your community for personal assistance work and decide if you are going to offer the benefits of housing and/or food. You may have to be assertive and creative in your outreach efforts to find a personal assistant, as oftentimes registries are not very reliable.

ADVERTISING

Depending on your style, you may find it helpful to develop a brief job description. This will require you to think through and write down exactly what you want an assistant to do. This is the point where you take your needs assessment and turn it into a series of descriptions of what you want and expect from your personal assistant.

Things to Think About:

Are you looking for someone to work part or full-time, to lift you, to assist you in grooming, in toileting, in feeding, in turning you over at night?

Note: If you're looking for someone to lift you, this should be included in the announcement along with the weight that an applicant must be able to lift.

- Do you want your assistant to help prepare your meals, clean your place, do your shopping, drive you places?
- Do you want a live-in assistant or just someone to come at specific times?
- Do you want a back-up assistant or two or three?

You will need to think about the best places to do your recruiting. Many young people believe that college and university campuses are smart places to recruit personal assistants, because students are always looking for part-time work. Some think that hospitals, medical facilities or medical clinics are fertile recruiting grounds. You may want to post on church, store, youth center, senior center, fitness center, or other high traffic bulletin boards in your community.

How to advertise is as important as where to advertise. A successful ad must:

- Be concise in wording (short and to the point).
- Explain specifically what you expect the person to do for you.

Don't:

- List your full name, address, and telephone number. You may receive unwanted calls or visits.
- Put too much information in the ad. Details can wait until the interview.
- Use jargon or acronyms that the general public may not understand.

The ad can be run in a local newspaper, posted on a bulletin board or the Internet, posted at local colleges and universities, or placed in a church or other organization's newsletter. An ad in a newspaper or a newsletter may cost per word or letter, so you will want your ad to be short.

Below are samples of an Internet ad and flyer.

Sample Internet Ad

Flexible Part-Time Job: Woman in Rockville Needs Personal Assistant (AM/PM shifts)

Reply to: job-xxxxxxxxx@craigslist.org
Date: 2008-11-20, 2:40 PM EST

Looking for some extra cash?
Consider becoming a Personal Assistant
Disabled student needs assistance with activities of daily living (i.e., showering, dressing, etc.) in the mornings (6:00-8:00 a.m.), evenings (6:30-8:00 p.m. and/or 9:00-11:30 p.m.), and on weekends (throughout the day). Looking for 2-4 people.

- No experience/special certifications necessary
- Must have a permit to work in the U.S. and be proficient in English
- Must have own transportation
- Must be able to lift at least 100 lbs.

- Must be punctual and reliable
- No age requirement
- Professional references required
- Must like dogs

Location: Washington, DC/Arlington, VA
Compensation: $12.50/hr

This is a part-time job.
Principals only. Recruiters, please don't contact this job poster.

Please, no phone calls about this job!
Please do not contact job poster about other services, products or commercial interests.

PostingID: 905523495

Sample Flyer

Live-in Assistant Sought

Free Room & $1,300 a month.
I am an active young female with neuromuscular weakness. I use a power chair and am independent during the day.

I need an assistant to help with personal care for about an hour each morning and evening. You must be able to fully carry a 105 lb. person for transfers.

For more information, please call Jane at (xxx) xxx-xxxx or e-mail me at xxxxxx@xxxx.com.

WRITING A JOB DESCRIPTION

A job description can be particularly useful if you find you're getting quite a few requests for more details about the position, or you want to make sure you're sharing the same level of detail with everyone who calls. It may also be beneficial if others are helping to spread the word about your need. Drafting the document means thinking through and writing down the exact duties of an assistant. For example:

MASON'S STORY

"For me, before I interview people, I make an in-depth job description so they know everything about the job," Mason explains. "Others have told me not to be so detailed because I should leave it until they come to do the job. But, I think they need to know the intricacies of where they have to bathe, etc., because I don't want them to leave when they discover they have to do some of the more personal things."

- Are you looking for someone to work part or full time, to lift you, to assist you in grooming, in toileting, in feeding, in turning you over at night?

- Do you want your assistants to help prepare your meals, clean your place, do your shopping, drive you places?

- Do you want a live-in assistant or just someone to help at specific times of day?

- Do you want one or more back-up assistants?

This is the point where you turn your needs assessment into a series of descriptions of what you want and expect from your personal assistant.

Personal Assistant
In the Chicago, IL Area

Thanks for your interest in the position. Let me tell you a little bit about what's involved. I have cerebral palsy and use an electric wheelchair. Because of my disability, I am unable to do many daily activities on my own, such as getting out of bed, dressing, showering, and transferring to my wheelchair. I would need assistance with these activities and others.

Requirements:
Although no experience is necessary, you must be able to lift about 90 lbs. I, or one of my current personal assistants, would show you how all these things are done--no need to worry!!!!!

Female
No experience/special certifications necessary
Must have a permit to work in the U.S.
Must have own transportation
Must be able to lift at least 90 lbs.
Must be punctual and reliable
No age requirement

Approximate Times (somewhat flexible) and General Tasks:
The number of hours an individual works is up to them. Generally, I have between four and five assistants working for me at one time. This allows for people to work as many hours as they would like. Usually, one person will work 3 to 4 days a week (i.e., Tuesday/Thursday mornings, and Friday afternoon).

The type of help I would need depends on the time of day. My personal assistants do not stay with me the entire day; instead they help me at certain times of the day: early morning, around noon, at dinnertime, and at bedtime. Below is an example of my schedule and the types of things I would need done at those times.

The morning time is basically set, because I work full-time. The other times are approximate and can be adjusted, if necessary. Weekend times are also somewhat flexible.

Weekdays
5:15-7:15 a.m.: Getting up, dressed, and ready for work. (1.5-2.0 hrs.)
6:00-7:30 p.m.: Going to the restroom, and possibly getting something to eat. (1-1.5 hrs.)
9:00-11:00 p.m.: Taking a shower and preparing for the next day. (1.5-2.0 hrs.)

Weekends
7:00-9:00 a.m.: Getting up, dressed, and ready. (1.5-2.0 hrs.)
11:30 a.m.-12:30 p.m. Going to the restroom, and possibly getting something to eat. (.5-1.0 hr.)
6:00-7:30 p.m.: Going to the restroom, and possibly getting something to eat. (1-1.5 hrs.)
10:00-11:30 p.m.: Taking a shower and preparing for the next day. (1.5-2.0 hrs.)

The initial screening will be one of your most important steps. The point is to be sure that you are sorting through the inappropriate callers. Think about the easiest way for you to screen potential applicants and handle requests for more information. How will potential candidates contact you? How much information do you want to provide over the telephone or in an e-mail?

When potential personal assistants call to discuss the job, you should have them tell you about themselves, why they are interested in the job, and what made them decide to call you. Have them do all the talking at first. Once you have a sense that they are serious, share the specific requirements of the job and ask if they understand or have any issues performing the tasks. Ask them open-ended questions, rather than questions that elicit simple "yes" or "no" answers. You want to be able to get as much information from them on the telephone as possible to decide whether they should be invited into your home. If all their questions are about money, hours, and/or benefits, then you will know that you are not their primary interest. Be consistent with each caller; that is, make sure you're asking similar initial questions and then delving deeper into issues that pique your interest.

And, as odd as it may seem, do not end the telephone call by setting up an interview time and date. Let them know you are accepting applications and will get back to them. You might want to e-mail them your job application, so they can fill it out and return it to you. You don't want to look desperate. Remember, most employers do not offer the job on the first telephone call. Be sure to get their telephone number before you hang up so you can call them back.

CLAIRE'S STORY

"It takes a lot of trust to have so many people coming and going in your home, so many people with keys to your place, coming at night and in the early mornings," Claire explains. Like many others who need assistance with their daily activities, Claire doesn't allow just anyone to have access to her place. "I'll screen out people by asking people if they can pass a background test. People are generally really honest," she recalls. "I had one person tell me he had a felony. People are really honest, and I'm a good judge of character."

Telephone Interview Checklist

Checklist for Telephone Interview

Information to Share:

- [ ] Your disability
- [ ] A general job description, including duties, days/times that you will need assistance
- [ ] When (during the day, during the week, etc.) you will need his/her services
- [ ] Your general location
- [ ] Your smoking preferences (i.e., Can a personal assistant smoke in your apartment?)
- [ ] Whether or not you have a service animal or pets (i.e., Is the potential personal assistant allergic to cats, dogs, or other types of animals?)
- [ ] Salary and method of payment (i.e., How much will you pay? What will be the average number of hours? How often will you pay your personal assistants? Will you pay them directly with a personal check or through some other method?)
- [ ] What you're looking for in a personal assistant (i.e., Are you interested in a friendly relationship/hanging out or a more professional relationship?)
- [ ] Some of your likes and dislikes as they relate to the personal assistant (i.e., Do you like to play loud music when a personal assistant is there, or do you need your home to be very quiet?)

Questions to Ask:

Tell me about your experiences with persons with disabilities:

_____

Things to Consider When Asking This Question:

There are pros and cons to hiring someone with experience. While someone who has worked as a personal assistant before may require less training, they may also come with preconceived ideas about how things should be done.

Tell me about your other work experiences:

_____

Things to Consider When Asking This Question:

Has the candidate moved from job to job? If so, ask why. This could be an indication you'll be training someone who won't be around for long. What are things they liked or didn't like about their other jobs? Will some of the same skills be required here (e.g., getting up early, working on weekends)? Did they like working with people?

Why are you interested in this job?

_____

Things to Consider When Asking This Question:

You want to pay close attention to not only what they say, but also how they say it. Are their first and only concerns/questions related to money? This could be a red flag. In any job interview, issues of money/salary should be some of the last questions. Besides, if it was mentioned in the ad, the applicant should have some idea of what to expect.

What is your current schedule, and how would this work fit into it?

Things to Consider When Asking This Question:

If the candidate has other commitments, will they interfere with providing you with the services you require? How far will they have to travel to get to you? If a person has only a little bit of flexibility in their schedule, this may impact the flexibility you have in getting their assistance.

Do you have reliable transportation?

Things to Consider When Asking This Question:

If they are relying on others for transportation, this could present problems in the long run. Will the personal assistant's driver wait outside or inside your home if s/he arrives before the personal assistant is ready to leave? Are you wiling to have individuals in your home unsupervised?

Everyone who works as a personal assistant must pass a criminal background check. Would this be a problem for you and are you comfortable with this?

Things to Consider When Asking This Question:

If the potential personal assistant expresses any hesitation or refusal to submit to a background check, this should be a red flag for you. If s/he readily offers information that may come up in the process of a background check, but insists that s/he made every effort to change, it is up to you to determine your comfort level. It may be helpful to consider both the nature of the offense and the type of help you will need. For example, if the offense is stealing/forging a check and your personal assistants have access to your bank account and checks, seeking counsel from your friends or family may be helpful in making a decision whether or not to hire the person. At the very least, you may want to consider requesting two additional professional/personal references.

Do you have any questions about the job that haven't been answered?

Things to Consider When Asking This Question:

In any job interview, it's seen as appropriate and beneficial to ask at least one question, even if there is very little that has been left unsaid. Asking questions demonstrates a genuine interest in the position.

If you are interested in meeting someone for an in-person interview, be sure to have all of her/his relevant contact information (i.e., name, phone number, e-mail). Set up a specific interview time and place for the interview, and ask the interviewee to please call at least one day ahead of time if s/he needs to cancel the meeting. Also, be sure to let the interviewee know if you would like her/him to bring any additional information or documents (i.e., copy of resume, references, etc).

INTERVIEWING CANDIDATES FACE-TO-FACE

If you think the applicant may be a good fit, arrange for a face-to-face interview. Initially, it may not seem like this type of interview is that much different than the phone interview, but don't discount the wealth of information that you can gather from watching and interacting with someone in person. A potential personal assistant's body language, facial expressions, attentiveness, and talkativeness will often provide clues as to how s/he will interact with you on a daily basis. The in-person interview should also be seen as an opportunity to determine whether the applicant can physically perform the required duties and whether your personalities are compatible.

CREATING THE JOB APPLICATION

You may want to develop a formal application to serve as a written record of details needed for tax and reference purposes. The application also provides a good starting point for the in-person interview and a means of comparing two or more applicants.

- Setting up a filing system can be useful in helping you keep records of applicants, whether you hire them or keep their application for future openings. There are at least four basic types of information that should be included on your application:

- Personal information such as full name, permanent address (not just a school address), home and cell phone numbers, and e-mail address;

- Employment history, including job, duties, employer, dates employed, and reasons for leaving;

- Complete contact information for at least the last three places the candidate worked, including employer, supervisor's name, position, telephone number, and e-mail address; and,

- Complete contact information for between two and five personal references, including name, relationship, telephone number, and e-mail address.

You may also want to ask them to write a short paragraph about why they want the job. This could help you remember people and give you a basis for asking some more detailed questions during the interview.

Remember that the job application is for your use. If you don't take the time to study the answers, you could be in for a big surprise. Blank portions or those with partial or vague information should be a red flag. Since the application contains information you'll need if you want to hire the candidate, make sure s/he fills it out before the interview.

Meeting Applicants

It may be best to arrange to meet in a public place near your home or even in the lobby of your apartment building, especially as you are still trying to determine whether the person is a good fit.

If meeting in your home is the only option, consider having a friend or family member present. You should still be the one conducting the interview, but having another person's perspective of the interviewee can sometimes be helpful. It can be useful to watch how the interviewee acts with another person present. For example, do they talk to you directly or talk to the friend/family member about you? You want to make sure the person talks to you directly.

A few general things you should keep in mind during the application and interview process:

- ✓ Did the person respond in a timely manner?

- ✓ Did s/he provide all the requested information?

- ✓ Did s/he show up for the interview on time?

- ✓ Was s/he actively engaged in the interview (not checking their watch, cell phone, or looking around the room)?

- ✓ Did s/he seem interested in what you had to say, and did s/he ask appropriate questions?

- ✓ Is the candidate open and willing to share some personal information without sharing too much?

- ✓ Does the candidate seem to treat you the same way s/he would anyone else your age —i.e., not talking down to you?

- ✓ Does the interviewee seem ready and willing to help in the short time you interact—i.e., willing to assist when needed?

JEFF'S STORY

When their son Jeff was very young, Raechelle and her husband learned about PAS through The ARC (at the time known as the Association for Retarded Children), a local community-based nonprofit organization that is part of a national affiliate network of similar organizations providing programs and services for children and youth with significant disabilities. They learned about respite care services, where assistants would come into their home and provide the PAS to give the parents a break from such routines.

"Since then, we have been in charge of training each personal assistant who works with Jeff," Raechelle says. "Now, we use agencies that take care of performing the initial screenings of personal assistants and sending the candidates for interviews. The agencies take care of paying and, though it hasn't been necessary, firing the assistants."

Both your questions and the information you provide about the job should be much more detailed than during the telephone interview. For example, if you weigh 150 pounds and need assistance transferring from your bed to a wheelchair, make sure the interviewee knows that. Also, if you have specific care needs like bathing or a bowel program, that information should be conveyed clearly to avoid potential problems in the future.

Evaluating Applicants

A critical part of the interview process is evaluating the applicant's ability to adequately perform the job duties described in the ad. Although it may seem like most people could do what you need done by a personal assistant, this is not always the case. Some people may be uncomfortable helping with very personal tasks, others may not like animals, and still others may be uncomfortable interacting with people with disabilities. These types of things are much easier to hide over the phone than in person.

It's important to ask a lot of personal questions, so you can get a good handle on whether or not the applicant is responsible and trustworthy. Be sure you are being honest and explicit about your needs. Take them on a tour of your home, explaining the critical aspects of the job. During the interview, you may want to have them demonstrate their ability to perform some of the required tasks.

Remember, you will be spending a lot of time with this person. You do not need to be best friends, but you should probably be able to have a basic conversation and enjoy each other's company. Also, communicate that confidentiality is expected regarding your personal information (i.e., what care they provide for you).

Following-Up With References and Background Checks

If you like a candidate, ask them for references from prior employers or persons who can attest to their integrity, responsibility, and character. One of the most important steps in the hiring process is taking the time to check backgrounds and call references. Most people who do not take the time

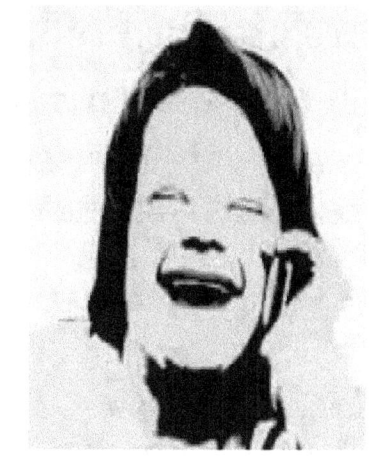

to do these things regret it later. You can hold off on doing the checks until after the interview or do them as an additional screen before the interview.

Background checks can help reveal a criminal record that did not come up in the initial screening. You can find out criminal background records by contacting your county law enforcement office or even checking online. The criminal records should be public information.

A driving record can also reveal valuable information about an individual's level of responsibility and safety, particularly if the individual has a negative driving record. You may be charged a small fee to gain access to this information, but the investment will help ensure your safety and peace of mind. You may need a release form to get the information from the Department of Motor Vehicles (DMV). This should be part of your application.

In-Person Interview Sample Questions

Checklist for In-Person Interview

Questions to Ask the Interviewee

Have you ever worked as a personal assistant before? Where? How long?

Things to Consider When Asking This Question:
A person doesn't necessarily need previous experience to be a good personal assistant. In fact, some people prefer to hire individuals that have no prior experience working with people with disabilities, so they come with no preconceived ideas about what will work best. If they have served as a personal assistant before, it's useful to determine how long they were in the position and their reasons for leaving.

What is your experience with people with disabilities?

Things to Consider When Asking This Question:
Again, it is not necessary that an individual have previous experience working with people with disabilities. You need to determine your own preferences in this area. For some, the greater questions are "Is this person willing to learn?" and "Do they treat me as an individual capable of making my own choices and decisions?" You may be able to determine the answers to these questions based on their descriptions of previous interactions with people with disabilities.

Why are you interested in being a personal assistant?

Things to Consider When Asking This Question:
This question serves as a good indicator of whether the person has realistic expectations of the job. If they are looking for a position that will help them pay their way through school and you are only able to give them 10 hours of work, being a personal assistant should probably not be the primary job for them. Be wary of someone who quickly agrees to take on as many hours as possible. Sometimes people are so interested in helping that they fail to look realistically at their own limitations to fulfill the job duties. In cases like this, urge the applicant to take several days to consider what s/he can handle, given his/her other responsibilities.

Are you looking for temporary or permanent work?

Things to Consider When Asking This Question:
You should consider how often you want to be looking for personal assistants. Are you interested in hiring someone only for a few months? Or, are you looking for someone to help you longer term?

What other jobs have you had?

Things to Consider When Asking This Question:
Asking for a resume may not be a bad idea. It will give you an opportunity to look at the individual's work history and ask questions. For example, has the applicant moved often between jobs, staying no more than a couple of months at a time? Does the individual have previous work experience that required a moderate or significant level of responsibility?

What did you like or dislike about those jobs?

Things to Consider When Asking This Question:
Are there aspects of being a personal assistant that are similar to the dislikes s/he has had related to other jobs? For example, s/he is not a morning person, and you're searching for someone to fill several morning slots.

Why did you leave those jobs?

Things to Consider When Asking This Question:
Knowing why an individual left a job can provide great insight as to whether they are willing and able to work through small issues/ big concerns. It can also indicate how dedicated the person is to staying in a particular job situation, even when there are challenges/difficulties.

[Discuss in detail the duties the assistant would perform.] Do any of these tasks make you uncomfortable? Why?

Things to Consider When Asking This Question:
It's important for your personal assistants to feel comfortable with the required tasks. If they are not, it may be best to consider other applicants for the job. Remember that you are hiring individuals to help you with your daily activities. While it's important to be flexible at times, you should not compromise your health or general well-being to accommodate others.

Do you prefer a job that is highly structured or one that is more flexible?

Things to Consider When Asking This Question:
Consider your own needs and preferences. Do you function best when your schedule is highly structured or more flexible? Do the applicant's preferences match your own?

How do you like to receive feedback from your employer?

Things to Consider When Asking This Question:
Does the applicant do better with oral or written instructions/feedback? It's best to determine that sooner rather than later. This will give you a better understanding of the best way to train an applicant, either through written instruction or by watching another assistant.

What would you do during "down time" on the job?

Things to Consider When Asking This Question:
Avoid having to pay someone for being with you when s/he is not doing anything. There may be times an assistant will have to wait for you (as you finish dinner, or are running late to meet him/her). Is the applicant a self-starter? In either case, it may be helpful to leave a to-do list in plain sight.

What is the biggest mistake you made in your last job? How did you correct the problem?

Things to Consider When Asking This Question:
Does the applicant readily share an instance when they made a mistake? It's important that the individual be able to take instruction/correction from you, especially as s/he learns what works best. A good personal assistant is usually confident enough to try new things, but not overconfident/overbearing.

Do you have your own transportation?

Things to Consider When Asking This Question:
If the interviewee does not have his/her own transportation, this may present a problem. For example, if s/he relies on public transportation or family/friends, you will have to coordinate an additional schedule. You may also have to adjust the time that you get help to accommodate two schedules.

What hours and days are you available?

Have available the Sample Weekly Schedules developed in the section of this manual on *Identifying What You're Looking for in a Personal Assistant.*

Everyone who works as a personal assistant must pass a criminal background check. Are you comfortable with this?

Things to Consider When Asking This Question:
Even if you asked this question during the phone interview, it's not a bad idea to ask again. If the potential personal assistant expresses any hesitation or refusal to submit to a background check, this should be a red flag for you. If s/he readily offers information that may come up in the process of a background check, but insists that s/he made every effort to change, it is up to you to determine what you are comfortable with. It may be helpful to consider both the nature of the offense and the type of help you will need. For example, if the offense is stealing/forging a check and your personal assistants have access to your bank account and checks, seeking counsel from your friends or family may be helpful in making a decision of whether to hire the person. At the very least, consider requesting two additional professional/personal references.

Sample Job Application

Job Application

Personal Information

Name: Today's Date:

School Address (if applicable):

Permanent Address:

Phone Number: (Home)   (Cell)   Best Time to Call:

Birth Date: Age: Social Security Number:

Valid Driver's License: Name of College and Major (if applicable):

Why are you interested in this job?

Last 3 Jobs (beginning with the most recent)

Name of Employer: Supervisor's Name:

Supervisor's E-mail and Phone Number:

Dates Worked: Reason for Leaving:

Name of Employer: Supervisor's Name:

Supervisor's E-mail and Phone Number:

Dates Worked: Reason for Leaving:

Name of Employer: Supervisor's Name:

Supervisor's E-mail and Phone Number:

Dates Worked: Reason for Leaving:

List 3 References (no relatives)

Name: E-mail:

Phone Number: Relationship:

Name: E-mail:

Phone Number: Relationship:

Name: E-mail:

Phone Number: Relationship:

CONTACTING REFERENCES

Because of the intimate nature of your relationship with a personal assistant, you'll definitely want to check their references before hiring. These references can be with both past employers and with friends or other social relations that can vouch for the individual's character. You can also determine whether the candidate has been truthful during the interview if the references confirm or contradict any of the candidate's statements.

Contacting the references can be uncomfortable, but it is essential for making a good hiring decision. If you call the reference, listen not only to what is said, but also how it is communicated. Does the reference hesitate? Does s/he answer questions directly?

Sample Questions for Applicant's Professional References
Checklist for Interview with Employment References

Information to Tell the Interviewee About You
- Introduce yourself
- Explain your disability and the need for a personal assistant
- Describe what the job involves

Questions to Ask Employment Reference

How long did [Applicant's Name] work for you?

_____

Was [Applicant's Name] dependable?

_____

Do you consider [Applicant's Name] to be honest?

_____

How does [Applicant's Name] respond to directions being given by a supervisor?

_____

Would you hire [Applicant's Name] again?

_____

Sample Questions for Applicant's Personal References
Checklist for Interview With Personal References

Information to Tell the Interviewee About You

- Introduce yourself
- Explain your disability and the need for a personal assistant
- Describe what the job involves

Questions to Ask Personal Reference

What is your relationship with [Applicant's Name]?

_____

How long have you known [Applicant's Name]?

_____

In your opinion, is [Applicant's Name] trustworthy?

_____

Would you want [Applicant's Name] to work for you if you were in my situation?

_____

Are there any outstanding things, either positive or negative, I should know about [Applicant's Name] before hiring him/her?

_____

SIGNING A CONTRACT

In all the forms and worksheets provided in this manual, you are encouraged to adapt them to your needs and circumstances. However, because an employment contract establishes a legal relationship and each state has established its own requirements for such a relationship, please consult a local resource center before using this form. Web sites for finding such centers are provided in the *Additional Resources* section.

Sample Contract

PERSONAL ASSISTANT   EMPLOYER

Name: Name:

Address: Address:

Phone: Phone:

Social Security #:

The above parties agree as follows:

1. Employer will require and Personal Assistant will provide _____ personal assistant hours per week with the following general services provided (and others as needed):

a)   b)

c)   d)

e)   f)

g)   h)

i)   j)

2. The Personal Assistant will maintain a regular weekly schedule as follows, with possible adjustments as needed and indicated with advance notice.

Monday: _____

Tuesday: _____

Wednesday: _____

Thursday: _____

Friday: _____

Saturday: _____

Sunday: _____

3. The following payment schedule has been agreed upon:
The cost for the Personal Assistant services provided herein is $_____ per hour multiplied by _____ hours per week multiplied by _____ weeks.

4. The Personal Assistant shall be paid on the following schedule:

_____

5. It is the responsibility of the Personal Assistant to submit the record of hours worked on the schedule specified above.

6. If the Personal Assistant is unable to fulfill the job duties or meet the above terms, s/he can be terminated. The Personal Assistant also understands that s/he may be terminated if the Employer no longer needs assistance, if interpersonal problems develop, or for any other reason the Employer may find.

7. Each party furthermore understands and agrees that the exact number of Personal Assistant hours per week may vary from week to week depending on Employer needs and that advance notice must be given if either party desires to terminate or modify this contract.

PERSONAL ASSISTANT SIGNATURE: EMPLOYER SIGNATURE:

_____   _____

DATE: DATE:

_____   _____

MANAGING A PERSONAL ASSISTANT

Getting Started

Now that you are the employer, it's important to manage your assistants and yourself. Consistency, open communication and clear direction will be critical. Always go back to your job description and your previously established rules. If you change any tasks or rules, be sure to talk them through with your assistant(s). Many issues will arise, so you and your assistant(s) will need to have good communication. This may include things like borrowing food, money, or clothes. None of these are a good idea, but if you do allow any of them, make sure the terms are clear. If your assistant(s) show up to work on drugs or drunk, address the issue immediately. And, be cautious about getting romantically or sexually involved with an assistant.

MASON'S STORY

"The only training I got was 'don't call your personal assistant names and say 'thank you,'" Mason recounts. "I got no training in how to tell your personal assistants that they need to be more respectful of me or how to do their job properly. Frankly, I'm still learning." He continues, "I want to be dressed a certain way. I have a complex that if I look at myself in a mirror and don't think I look good, people will look at and treat me differently. If people see me dressed nicely, sitting up straight in my chair, they will think 'oh, he really tries hard.' Most personal assistants don't realize that it's my image. They just think it's about putting my shirt on."

MAKING NEW EMPLOYEES FEEL WELCOME

It's important that both you and your new employee feel comfortable with each other. Starting a new job can be stressful and overwhelming. Making the personal assistant feel welcome from day one will motivate him/her to do a good job supporting you. Here are a few suggestions:

- ✔ Invite the new personal assistant to sit and talk with you about the new role.
- ✔ Go over the personal assistant's schedule and talk about what you want him/her to do.
- ✔ Show the personal assistant around your home. Point out where important things are like the phone and the bathroom.
- ✔ Introduce the personal assistant to the important people in your life, such as family and friends.
- ✔ Talk about the rules of the house, such as when it's okay for them to use the phone for personal use, and where they can eat.
- ✔ Talk about what you like and don't like, as well as how you spend your time.
- ✔ Remind him/her that confidentiality is expected.
- ✔ Share your schedule and routine.

You want to have a friendly relationship with your personal assistant, but you also need to remember that s/he is now your employee—and you need to consider how to become an effective employer. For each task, be very clear from the beginning about how you would like it done. Otherwise, the personal assistant will not be aware of your preferences.

For example, assistants may do your laundry the way they do their own. So, if you have certain preferences, be specific. This should be the case in all tasks—even the most basic (e.g., dishes, food preparation, and housecleaning). You may want to consult the worksheets in the *Identifying What You Want and Need in a Personal Assistant* section to help decide what to communicate to your personal assistant. Clear communication with your personal assistant will help him/her do the job effectively, which will ultimately make you happier. Communication is critical to a strong, successful employer/employee relationship. Discuss concerns or problems as they develop. The longer you avoid discussing them, the harder and more difficult working together becomes.

Another important piece of any working relationship is respect. Mutual respect is essential to helping your assistant feel like a valued employee. You will also earn more respect from your employee if you actively show him/her respect and appreciation.

CLAIRE'S STORY

Claire learned how to manage her personal assistants through the college disability program as well as from her local independent living center. "I learned a lot from the personal one-on-one conversation with the counselor," she says. "Talking with friends on campus helped a lot, too."

HANDLING AWKWARD MOMENTS

No one likes awkward situations. In fact, most people try to avoid them. Chances are, though, that if you rely on someone else for assistance with your daily activities, you will undoubtedly experience more than your fair share of awkward moments. It's important to think about how you

MASON'S STORY

"Be direct in what you need," advises Mason. "Be sure you know who you are. Your assistant may be the same age, may be older. There may be something that needs to be talked about." Some people "don't like being told what to do," he acknowledges. He believes, in cases like that, someone should not be an assistant. "When I have to ask for every little move, every little touch, every turn," he explains, "I get frustrated. I know it sounds bossy, but it's just the way it is."

will address these situations. Having someone else see you naked, bathe you, change your tampon, wipe you, or any other personal task is bound to be awkward until you and your personal assistant reach a comfort level about those private tasks. You may need to make sure your personal assistant is truly getting you clean when they wipe your behind or change your menstrual pad. You may find sensitive touches sexually arousing. You may be surprised at how your body responds during such private moments. Your personal assistant may be shocked, embarrassed, or offended if your body responds in a sexual fashion.

Similarly, you need to understand that you are the employer and the personal assistant is the employee. Sometimes, as people begin to feel attracted to and romantically inclined toward their assistant, they find themselves wanting more than PAS. Certainly, there are lots and lots of stories where someone with a disability fell in love with and married his or her assistant; regardless, you and your personal assistant will need to address those awkward moments and changes in your relationship should they occur. You may also just want your personal assistant to be your friend, as s/he is a person who spends quite a bit of time with you. These moments will arise, and your preparation for them in advance is advisable.

TRAINING YOUR PERSONAL ASSISTANTS

Training is one of the most important parts of managing your personal assistant(s). You are the expert when it comes to knowing your needs. Even experienced personal assistants need to be trained in how you want things done. If you have had personal assistants before, you probably already have a good idea of what works for you.

There is more than one way to train personal assistants. Some people respond well to oral directions, while others learn better from hands-on demonstrations. You may prefer training your own personal assistant by yourself or having one of your experienced personal assistants help with the training. Some people prefer to have their Qualified Professional do the training. Whatever method you use, these three steps are helpful:

✓ Have the personal assistant watch your morning or evening routine;

✓ Have the personal assistant perform that routine with an experienced personal assistant present. Repeat the routine until the personal assistant feels comfortable working directly with you; and

✓ Work directly with the personal assistant (expecting that each personal assistant is going to forget steps in the routine and just needs to be reminded).

If you are training a new personal assistant, here are things you may want to do:

- Talk about your disability and how it affects your life. The more your personal assistant knows about your disability, the better s/he will be able to meet your needs.

- Give a lot of examples and explain any technical terms you use.

- Try to consistently enforce the little things in the beginning, especially things that matter to you. Preventing bad work habits is easier than correcting them.

- Talk about any symptoms or health concerns. Discuss possible scenarios that may arise and how to handle them. For example, if you have epilepsy, what can the personal assistant do when you are having a seizure?

- As you go through your routine, explain the reason for certain tasks. This will help personal assistants realize the importance of these tasks. For example, if you do range of motion exercises, explain that they help maintain movement and flexibility.

- Provide training on how to operate any life support equipment (e.g., feeding tubes, ventilators, etc.), including properly handling and cleaning this equipment or any other medical supplies.

- Be patient. Learning how to do new things takes a while. Don't become frustrated if your personal assistant does not catch on right away.

- Be flexible and willing to compromise, but always remain in control of the situation.

- Ask for feedback about how you are explaining things. Maybe there is a way you could be clearer in your explanations.

- Stress the importance of documentation of tasks and times.

You can also organize your home and/or your schedule to make the training both faster and more effective. For example, you may color code drawers so that the personal assistant can easily locate specific items. If you are hiring more than one personal assistant, consider separating the duties among them rather than have one assistant do all the work at the time. That way, each personal assistant learns fewer job duties, which can expedite training.

Supplying written guidelines is also important. A set of written guidelines provides the personal assistant with clear instructions, and you with legal evidence in the event you face a legal battle for terminating a personal assistant for not meeting these terms. An example of written guidelines is presented below.

By providing good training up front, you may increase the chances of a personal assistant being able to be more effective at his/her job. Taking more time at the beginning can lead to better overall results.

Sample PA Guidelines and Policies

Personal Assistant Guidelines and Policies

Over the years, I have had numerous personal assistants. The items explained below have all come up at one time or another, so I thought it would be best to provide written expectations. While I would like your work experience with me to be as informal and enjoyable as possible, I do feel it's necessary to establish some guidelines. Please read them carefully.

Changes in Schedule/Flexibility:

I am willing to make changes or adjustments in my schedule as well as yours. Please let me know if there are meetings, concerts, or other events (or other personal plans) you need or would like to attend. We may be able to adjust the time(s) that you come to help me. I would appreciate this same understanding from you.

In addition, I know that there can be changes in schedules. Please notify me as soon as possible, so that we can do everything necessary to accommodate your schedule as well as mine.

Days Off:

I ask that an assistant request days off at least one to two weeks in advance. In the case of holidays, serious illness, or death in the family, exceptions will be made. I ask that you find someone to cover your shifts if you would like time off. Names and numbers of my current personal assistants will be provided (with their approval). Under extenuating circumstances (i.e., not able to find a replacement and unable to work), please call me directly. I do ask that you give me as much notice as possible, so that I have adequate time to find a replacement, if for some reason you cannot. Days off are unpaid.

Sick Days:

If you can't come in because of an illness, I ask that you find a replacement. Unfortunately, no one can be healthy all the time, and getting sick is not something anyone can schedule or predict. I realize these things, but assistant care is essential to my daily functioning. Names and numbers of my current personal assistants will be provided (with their approval). Under extenuating circumstances (i.e., not able to find a replacement and unable to work), please call me directly. I do ask that you give me as much notice as possible, so that I have adequate time to find a replacement, if for some reason you cannot. As you may expect, you will not be paid for sick days.

Being Punctual/Tardiness:

Please make every effort to be punctual. As I have mentioned before, many of my day-to-day activities (i.e., getting up, going to the bathroom, or going to bed) hinge on assistance from personal assistants, and I consider my time just as valuable as yours. While there are sometimes unexpected delays, being late on a regular basis will be considered cause for termination. If you know you're going to be late, please try to notify me beforehand. Personal assistants who arrive more than 15 minutes late (without calling beforehand) will receive a verbal warning. Personal assistants who receive three or more verbal warnings may be asked to leave. Consistent calls will also be cause for termination.

Just as I have asked that you try to be punctual, please know that I will do the same. If possible, I will notify you in advance when I know I'll be late.

Phone/E-mail Use:

Personal assistants will be allowed to make very brief (5 minute) phone calls from work under certain circumstances. Since the time you will spend at work is often less than two hours at one time, please refrain from making personal calls while on-the-job. As always, there are exceptions. If you must make a call, please simply ask before doing so. This applies to both local and long-distance calls. Under no circumstances will personal assistants be allowed to make long-distance calls without using their own phone cards.

Meals:

Meals will not be provided to personal assistants who happen to work around meal times. Personal assistants are more than welcome to eat with me, provided they purchase their own meal. However, I will not pay personal assistants for the time they spend eating their meal.

Running Errands:

You will be paid for assisting me in running errands. This could include, but is not limited to, food shopping, doctor's appointments, or assisting me in getting to other appointments. In making appointments, I will consult you as to a good day and time (if I need assistance). You will be compensated for your time.

Smoking:

Please refrain from smoking while on-the-job. As I mentioned, the time you will spend at work is often less than two hours at one time. Therefore, I think it's reasonable to ask that you not smoke while at work. If you are concerned about this policy, please discuss this with me.

Leaving:

If it becomes necessary for you to leave this job, please give me at least four (4) weeks' notice. Ideally, I would like all my personal assistants to stay on-the-job as long as possible; nevertheless, I realize situations change. As you may know, finding an assistant takes some time, and it's not a decision I make lightly.

Probationary Period:

There will be a two-week probationary period. Sometimes it's difficult to tell if a person is the best fit for the job until they are actually in the job. After two weeks, there will be an informal assessment to determine how things are working for everyone.

Background Checks:

All applicants must be willing to submit to a background check, and provide the results to me. The cost will be reimbursed.

Terminations:

There are situations that will result in termination. Although firing a personal assistant is unpleasant, it is sometimes necessary. As mentioned before, habitual tardiness may result in termination (See *Being Punctual/Tardiness* for more details.) In addition, use of my phone to make long-distance calls, theft, forgery, working under the influence of alcohol or drugs, or use of my vehicle for personal errands will result in immediate termination. Under no circumstances will any of these actions be tolerated.

Payment of Personal Assistants:

Payment Schedule - It is your responsibility to turn in your timesheets, keep track of your hours, and notify me of your total hours worked. Please note that I also keep track of personal assistant hours for my benefit and yours. Failure to turn in a timesheet on time will affect your pay schedule.

Taxes - I will not take taxes out of your paycheck, but I do consider assistant care a medical expense on my own taxes. In other words, I report the money I pay you on my taxes. It is your responsibility to pay taxes on your income from this job. I suggest that you put some money aside as you get paid, so that you have money available when tax time rolls around.

Because I report this on my taxes, it's essential that you be able to legally work in the U.S. I will ask for documentation.

Please talk with an accountant for more information.

PAYING YOUR PERSONAL ASSISTANTS

One of the most critical parts of this process for you will be tracking the time worked by your assistant(s) and getting them paid on time.

As discussed earlier, various factors impact how your personal assistant costs will be covered. In addition, there are different laws, policies, and procedures that govern personal assistant compensation. Check with your local resource center to make certain you understand the rules in your area. Web sites for finding such centers are provided in the *Additional Resources* section of this toolkit. The way you handle keeping track of time will be extremely important for your reimbursement or voucher payment process with whomever is covering the costs of your personal assistance services. Make sure you know the reporting requirements of the funding source(s) and follow the rules strictly.

Whatever your situation, accurate records of employees' work hours are important for making sure they are paid appropriately. You may find it helpful to create a basic timesheet that can be transferable to anyone working with you as an assistant. This can get complicated if you have multiple funding sources and/or multiple assistants. It will be necessary to pay close attention to detail. Keep good, well-organized records. The following sample timesheet can be adapted based on specific requirements in your area. Make certain that both you and the personal assistant sign and date the timesheet and that you retain a copy in your records. Also, if you pay the personal assistant directly, it's a good idea to have the individual sign upon receiving each payment. This procedure will avoid confusion and potential problems later.

Your assistant will likely be eager to be paid on time. You will need to be very deliberate about any tax-related issues;

that is, whether you or the provider agency will pay taxes on the income earned by the employee, or if the employee will have that responsibility. Be clear about this with assistants from the get-go.

In addition to all the signed timesheets for your personal assistant(s), you will want to retain a file that includes:

- ✓ Contact information
- ✓ Signed job application
- ✓ Resume and references
- ✓ Signed employment agreement
- ✓ All written evaluations

Sample Timesheet

Weekly Timesheet

Name: _____

For Week of _____ through _____

Date	Hours
Sunday	
Monday	
Tuesday	
Wednesday	
Thursday	
Friday	
Saturday	

TOTAL FOR WEEK:

Employee Signature: _____ Date: _____

Employer Signature: _____ Date: _____

EVALUATING YOUR EMPLOYEES

It is important for personal assistants to know how they are performing and whether they are meeting your expectations. This can occur both informally with daily feedback and by doing a formal evaluation. It is recommended that you formally evaluate your personal assistant at least once a year and probably more often for new personal assistants.

To ensure an effective relationship with your personal assistant, give feedback often. Praise good performance and initiative. It will make the personal assistant(s) feel good and encourage continued good performance. Praise will also balance the times when you need to correct him/her.

Do not save praise or criticism for the evaluations. Evaluation is a formal review process and is done at least once a year. Feedback can happen on a daily basis. Personal assistants need to know how they are doing so they can continue to do things or change them. You may find giving such feedback uncomfortable—especially if you are criticizing the employee. Talk with others who have supervised personal assistants to get tips on doing this effectively.

Using an evaluation form can help structure the evaluation and serve to document job performance. The following sample evaluation form is provided for your use. When you adapt this for your own needs, include daily tasks, timeliness, and how you interact with one another.

Formal evaluations can help you remind your personal assistant(s) of his/her job duties and what is important to you. It is also a chance for your personal assistant(s) to give you feedback. There may be ways you can do things differently that would make it easier for your employees.

Keep copies of the evaluations in your personal assistant's file and give a copy to him/her. Review past evaluations when a personal assistant is having problems. Going over past evaluations can be helpful when you are thinking of firing an assistant. It may be a good reminder to see if there has been an ongoing problem and whether you have addressed it in past evaluations.

Some assistants may need more time to perform well. If feedback and evaluations do not improve performance, give a written warning that things need to improve by a certain date. Be sure to document this warning and put it in the personal assistant's file. If one warning doesn't work, you may issue a second warning. Again, it is important to write this down and put it in the personal assistant's file. After the second warning, make sure the personal assistant understands that things need to improve or s/he may be fired.

Sample Evaluation Form

Personal Assistant Evaluation Form

Attendance	Poor				Superior
	1	2	3	4	5
Follows Work Schedule					
Reports to Work on time					
No Excessive Absences					
Gives Appropriate Notice for Absences					

Performance	Poor				Superior
	1	2	3	4	5
Job Knowledge					
Follows Instructions					
Takes Initiative/Self-Starter					
Performs Tasks Thoroughly and in Timely Manner					

Behavior	Poor				Superior
	1	2	3	4	5
Demonstrates Respect for You and Your Ability to Make Decisions					
Takes Feedback/Open to Suggestions					
Communicates Well					
Positive Attitude					
Trustworthy					

Behavior	Poor			Superior
	1	2	3	4
Patience				
Willing to Learn				

Strengths

Recommendations for Improvement

Additional Training Needed

Ways to Strengthen Our Working Relationship

Other Comments

Employee Signature: _____ Date: _____

Employer Signature: _____ Date: _____

RECOGNIZING ABUSIVE SITUATIONS

Note: The following section of the toolkit is adapted from *Working Together: Personal Assistance Services Training and You* by the Center for Personal Assistance Services (http://www.pascenter.org/pas_users/index_pas.php): Personal Assistance Services User Manual, Independent Living Services Center, Everett, WA, http://fp.richpoor.com/ilsc/toc2ack.html

Just as a good personal assistant can enhance independence, a bad one can hinder it or be dangerous. It's important to recognize abusive situations and take steps to prevent or stop them. Abuse can come in many forms—physical, emotional, sexual, and financial. The word "abuse" typically brings to mind extreme physical abuse, but things like neglect or verbal abuse should be taken just as seriously.

Depending on your relationship with your personal assistants, it may be difficult to distinguish between joking and serious comments. Perhaps your assistant criticizes or teases you in a way that hurts your feelings. Maybe s/he tells you that you are "too demanding" or "too much trouble." While everyone experiences rough days, if this behavior persists, it may be an indication that there is more going on. Seek assistance from a friend, family member, or another adult you trust. And, if necessary, involve the authorities.

You, as the employer, can also take steps to protect yourself and stop the behavior before it escalates:

- Reiterate to your personal assistant that his/her behavior is disrespectful and inappropriate; and

- Advise your personal assistant that the behavior needs to stop if s/he wants to continue working for you.

Taking Additional Steps to Prevent Abuse

✓ Do thorough background and reference checks.

✓ Be careful about giving personal assistants access to your cash, checks, bank account, or credit cards. Consider leaving extra checks, bank statements, and other personal information in a locked file cabinet. If you need assistance accessing the cabinet, only allow one or two trusted personal assistants to open it with you present.

✓ Use your credit card only occasionally. This is one of the easiest ways for someone to steal from you.

✓ Implement personal assistant guidelines for using your property. This includes your car or van, telephone, and home. If you have a live-in personal assistant, establish guidelines regarding visitors and overnight guests, food, etc.

✓ If a personal assistant quits or is fired, be sure to get the keys back and give him or her the last paycheck. If the keys are not returned, have your locks changed immediately.

Evaluating Your Situation: Are You Being Abused?

Does your personal assistant...

Touch you or handle your body in a way that hurts or frightens you?	☐ Yes	☐ No
Refuse to give you the help you need to eat, dress, or go to the bathroom?	☐ Yes	☐ No
Hit you, slap you, or otherwise hurt you on purpose?	☐ Yes	☐ No
Hurt you by being careless when assisting you?	☐ Yes	☐ No
Prevent you from using important things like your glasses, hearing aid, medication, communication device, cane, or wheelchair?	☐ Yes	☐ No
Use belts or straps against your will to prevent you from moving?	☐ Yes	☐ No
Give you too much medication or deny you medication?	☐ Yes	☐ No
Do anything with physical force that may cause bodily injury or pain?	☐ Yes	☐ No
Ever touch you in a sexual way that makes you feel uncomfortable?	☐ Yes	☐ No
Ever pressure you to engage in any sexual acts?	☐ Yes	☐ No
Deny you sexual information or education (e.g., about birth control, childbirth)?	☐ Yes	☐ No
Force their opinions about abortion or sterilization on you?	☐ Yes	☐ No
Make suggestive comments or looks?	☐ Yes	☐ No
Ever threaten you, your loved ones, or your pets/service animal?	☐ Yes	☐ No
Call you names, make slurs about your nationality, ethnicity or color, or otherwise insult you?	☐ Yes	☐ No
Isolate you from friends and family?	☐ Yes	☐ No
Deny you the right to make personal decisions by making decisions for you?	☐ Yes	☐ No
Create anguish or distress through verbal or non-verbal acts?	☐ Yes	☐ No
Give you the "silent treatment"?	☐ Yes	☐ No
Harass you, willfully causing anxiety and distress?	☐ Yes	☐ No
Steal or intentionally damage things that belong to you?	☐ Yes	☐ No
Pressure you to spend money for things you really don't want?	☐ Yes	☐ No
Borrow money or anything else from you and not repay or return it you?	☐ Yes	☐ No
Deny you access to and control over your own money, misuse your credit cards or ATM cards, or mislead you about your accounts?	☐ Yes	☐ No
Pressure you to sign papers that you do not understand or have not read (such as Durable Power of Attorney), or put him/her on your bank account?	☐ Yes	☐ No
Ask for regular cash advances for unworked hours, then fail to show up for work?	☐ Yes	☐ No

Are you being neglected? Are you...

Being denied food or being provided food that you are not supposed to have? ☐ Yes ☐ No

Not getting the personal or medical care that you need? ☐ Yes ☐ No

If you answer "yes" to any of these questions, your personal assistant is being abusive towards you, though s/he may not be aware of it. These questions also apply to relationships and interactions you may have with anyone, not just your personal assistant.

FIRING YOUR PERSONAL ASSISTANT

Unfortunately, a time may come when you need to consider terminating a personal assistant. It is important to plan carefully for this situation, and to put a lot of thought into how you will approach it. Here are some common reasons for termination:

- Performance is not acceptable.
- The personal assistant is frequently late or does not show up for work.
- Personal habits bother you. For example, the personal assistant smokes while doing your care or has poor personal hygiene.
- The personal assistant does not listen to your instructions.
- You do not feel safe with the personal assistant, even though s/he has been working for you for several weeks and training has been provided.

When termination occurs, there is generally a two-week notice given. However, a personal assistant may need to be fired when his/her behavior endangers you or your property. In this case, it is unnecessary to give a two-week notice. Examples of gross misconduct that may require firing include:

- Physical or sexual assault or harassment (either at work or outside of working hours)
- Threatening behavior (to you or anyone else)
- Deliberately or knowingly endangering your safety or anyone else's
- Arriving under the influence of alcohol or illegal drugs Theft or fraud
- Deliberate damage to your property
- Verbal abuse (to you or anyone else)
- Breaking your confidentiality
- Gross insubordination (includes any conduct that
- tends to undermine your independence or self-determination)
- Failure to disclose criminal charges or convictions in their application form

Never fire a personal assistant on impulse while you are mad; the rationale for a valid firing is a clear list of well-established problems that cannot be resolved. If you decide to fire a personal assistant, here are some tips that may be helpful:

- For safety reasons, it is a good idea to have someone with you when you fire the personal assistant.
- Perform the firing at the end of the personal assistant's shift in order to minimize conflict.

Before the personal assistant arrives on the day of the firing, review the list of reasons that have made the firing absolutely necessary. Write out the list if you fear that your mind might go blank during the meeting.

- Be ready to give your reasons to the personal assistant in writing.

- Have a replacement personal assistant ready if at all possible. Make sure you have someone who can step in right away.

- Ask for keys to your home and any other personal property of yours the personal assistant may have. Consider changing your door locks.

- Be prepared for the personal assistant to be upset. Remain calm and avoid a confrontation.

- Be firm, but kind. Say that things are just not working out and while you both have tried, it is just not enough.

- Don't change your mind once you have decided. If you change your mind about firing the personal assistant, things may not improve and could get considerably worse.

ADDITIONAL RESOURCES

WEB SITES

Center for Personal Assistance Services: www.pascenter.org/home/index.php

Centers for Medicare and Medicaid Services: www.cms.hhs.gov/home/medicaid.asp

Community Living Exchange Collaborative: www.hcbs.org

Disability.gov: www.disability.gov

HSC Foundation's Youth Transitions Initiative: www.hscfoundation.org/whatwedo/youthtransitionsinitiative.php

Independent Living Centers: www.ilru.org

Kids as Self Advocates: www.fvkasa.org

National Collaborative on Workforce and Disability for Youth: www.ncwd-youth.info

National Council for Independent Living: www.ncil.org

National Disabled Students Union: www.disabledstudents.org

National Youth Leadership Network: www.nyln.org

PACER Center: www.pacer.org

Parent Resource Centers: www.taalliance.org

Supplemental Security Income: www.socialsecurity.gov/ssi/index.htm

University of Connecticut's Center for Students with Disabilities: www.csd.uconn.edu/personal_assistant_info.html

Vocational Rehabilitation Offices: www.ed.gov/about/offices/list/osers/rsa/index.html

BOOKS AND GUIDES

A Step-by-Step Guide to Training and Managing Personal Assistants: Consumer Guide
www2.ku.edu/~rtcil/products/RTCIL%20publications/Personal%20Assistance/PA%20Manual%20print%20version%20Consumer%20guide.pdf
Research and Training Center on Independent Living University of Kansas, March 2006

Avoiding Attendants from Hell: A Practical Guide to Finding, Hiring & Keeping Personal Care Attendants
June Price, 2001

CSU /DRC Personal Assistance Informational Manual: A Guide for Both Users of Personal Assistance and for Those Providing Personal Assistance
www.southernct.edu/drc/uploads/textWidget/wysiwyg/documents/PA_Informational_Manual.doc
Southern Connecticut State University's Disability Resource Center, 2008/2009

Enhancing Independence: A Consumer's Guide to Personal Assistance Services
Missouri Model Spinal Cord Injury System, University of Missouri-Columbia, 2005

Find, Choose & Keep Great DSPs: A Toolkit for People with Disabilities.
http://rtc.umn.edu/ildspworkforce/index.asp
University of Minnesota, Institute on Community Integration, Department of Disability and Human Development, 2006

Hiring and Management of Personal Care Assistants for Individuals with Spinal Cord Injury
www.tbi-sci.org/pdf/pas.pdf
Santa Clara Valley Medical Center

One Stop Toolkit for Serving People with Disabilities
www.onestoptoolkit.org/employment.cfm

PAS Facts: Finding a Workplace Personal Assistant
www.worksupport.com/documents/PASFACTSVol2.pdf
Ed Turner, 2007

Personal Assistance in the Workplace: A Customer-Directed Guide
www.worksupport.com/Main/pass.asp?CFID=13195509&CFTOKEN=31207497
Ed Turner, Grant Revell and Valerie Brooke

Personal Assistance Services Curriculum
www.bu.edu/cpr/resources/pas-curriculum/
Center for Psychiatric Rehabilitation, 2009

Personal Assistance Services (WPAS) in the Workplace
U.S. Department of Labor, Office of Disability Employment Policy, 2006

Working Together: Personal Assistance Training and You
www.infouse.com/pas/

OTHER

Web Cast: Personal Assistance Services in the Workplace
Lou Orslene, June 2005
www.worksupport.com/training/webcastDetails.cfm/26

Center for PAS Bulletin (quarterly)
The Center for Personal Assistance Services
www.pascenter.org/newsletter/index.php

GLOSSARY OF TERMS

Activities of Daily Living: These are things you do every day such as dressing, grooming, bathing, eating, positioning, transferring, and toileting.

Americans with Disabilities Act (ADA): (P.L. 101-336) The civil rights legislation prohibiting discrimination against people with disabilities. Public and private businesses, state and local government agencies, private entities offering public accommodations and services, transportation and utilities are required to comply with the law.

Assistance Dog: A generic term for guide, hearing, or service dog specifically trained to do more than one task to mitigate the effects of an individual's disability. The presence of a dog for protection, personal defense, or comfort does not qualify that dog as an assistance dog. (http://www.assistancedogsinternational.org/Standards/GlossaryOfTerms.php)

Assistive Technology: Assistive technology (or adaptive technology) is defined as including both the assistive technology devices and the services (e.g., repair and maintenance) needed to make meaningful use of such devices. The Assistive Technology Act defines an assistive technology device as: any item, piece of equipment, or product system, whether acquired commercially off the shelf, modified, or customized, that is used to increase, maintain, or improve functional capabilities of individuals with disabilities. An assistive technology service is defined as: any service that directly assists an individual with a disability in the selection, acquisition, or use of an assistive technology device. Assistive technologies are not workforce PAS.

Health-Related Functions: Services that must be delegated or assigned by a licensed health care professional, such as a nurse or doctor. Health-related functions are usually required to be provided under the direction of a qualified professional (QP) or a doctor. Examples of health-related functions are special skin care, non-sterile catheter care, tube feedings and respiratory assistance.

Home Health Agency: Home health agencies usually have a license from the Department of Health or other disability-related department and are Medicare-certified. These agencies typically provide skilled nursing visits, home health aide visits, occupational and physical therapy (OT/PT) visits, as well as PAS.

Instrumental Activities of Daily Living: These activities include personal hygiene, light housework, laundry, meal preparation, transportation, grocery shopping, using the telephone, medication management, and money management.

Major Bodily Functions: These include but are not limited to the operation of a major bodily function, including but not limited to, functions of immune system, normal cell growth, digestive, bowel, bladder, neurological, brain, respiratory, circulatory, endocrine, and reproductive functions.

Major Life Activities: Caring for oneself, performing mental tasks, seeing, hearing, eating, sleeping, walking, standing, lifting, bending, speaking, breathing, learning, reading, concentrating, thinking, communicating, and working.

Personal Assistance Services (PAS)

World Institute on Disability (WID) definition: Assistance, under maximum feasible user control, with tasks that maintain well-being, comfort, safety, personal appearance, and interactions within the community and society as a whole.

Medicaid Eligibility definition: Range of human assistance provided to persons with disabilities and chronic conditions of all ages, which enables them to accomplish tasks they would normally do for themselves if they did not have a disability.

Rehabilitation Act and the Ticket to Work and Work Incentives Improvement Act (TWWIIA) definition: A range of services provided by one or more persons designed to assist an individual with a disability to perform daily living activities on or off the job that the individual would typically perform if the individual did not have a disability. Such services shall be designed to increase the individual's control in life and ability to perform everyday activities on or off the job.

Personal Assistant (PA), Personal Care Assistant (PCA), or Attendant: Person who performs personal assistance services.

Personal Care Provider Organizations: Sometimes called PCA Agencies. These are community-based organizations or agencies that only provide PAS.

Reasonable Accommodation: A modification or adjustment to a job that enables a qualified individual with a disability to perform the job functions and thus enjoy equal employment benefits and privileges.

Service Dog: A dog that works for individuals with disabilities other than blindness or deafness. They are trained to perform a wide variety of tasks including but not limited to: pulling a wheelchair, bracing, retrieving, alerting to a medical crisis, and providing assistance in a medical crisis.

The Ticket to Work and Work Incentive Improvement Act: This landmark legislation modernizes the employment services system for people with disabilities and makes it possible for millions of Americans with disabilities to no longer have to choose between taking a job and having health care. The four sections of the Act that provide health care support for people with disabilities who work are:

Medicaid Buy-In. Section 201 of the Ticket to Work and Work Incentives Improvement Act governs the provision of health care services to workers with severe disabilities by establishing a Medicaid state plan buy-in optional eligibility group. As of 2008, more than 90,000 individuals in 40 states were covered under this new eligibility group.

Extended Medicare Coverage. Section 202 extends the period of premium free Medicare Part A coverage and requires consumer protection for some individuals with Medigap coverage. Individuals receiving Social Security Disability Insurance who elect to work above threshold levels (substantial gainful activity) can maintain their Medicare coverage for eight and a half years after they return to work.

Medicaid Infrastructure Grants. Section 203 provides grants to states to develop state infrastructures to support working individuals with disabilities. As of 2008, more than 40 states and the District of Columbia were participating in this program.

Demonstration to Maintain Independence and Employment. Section 204 provides health care coverage to individuals with potentially disabling conditions who work testing the hypothesis that the provision of health care and related supports will prolong independence and employment and reduce dependency on disability income support programs.

Workplace Personal Assistance Services: Task-related assistance at work, including readers, interpreters, and help with lifting or reaching. Non-essential tasks may also be re-assigned to co-workers. Workplace PAS might include personal care-related assistance, such as helping someone with eating, drinking, or using the restroom while at the job site.

REFERENCES

Americans with Disabilities Act of 1990, Pub.L. 101-336, 104 Stat. 327, (1990).

Assistance Dogs International, Inc. (ADI). (2009a). Glossary of Terms. Retrieved December 17, 2009, from http://www.assistancedogsinternational.org/Standards/GlossaryOfTerms.php

Assistance Dogs International, Inc. (ADI). (2009b). Realistic Answers to Frequently Asked Questions. Retrieved December 17, 2009, from http://www.assistancedogsinternational.org/Standards/GlossaryOfTerms.php

Equal Employment Opportunity Commission. (1992). A Technical Assistance Manual On The Employment Provisions (Title I) Of The Americans With Disabilities Act. Retrieved December 17, 2009, from http://www.jan.wvu.edu/links/ADAtam1.html#III

Holt, J., Chambless, C., & Hammond, M. (2006). Employment personal assistance services (EPAS), Journal of Vocational Rehabilitation, 24, 165-175.

Kraus, L. (2007). The ADA and Beyond: Reducing Barriers to PAS at Work. Summary Proceedings from the Meeting of the Nation's Needs for Personal Assistance Services State of the Science Conference, April 27, 2007, 11-12 http://www.pascenter.org/documents/SOS_Conf_Proceedings.pdf

Silverstein, R. (2003). The Applicability of the ADA to Personal Assistance Services in the Workplace. Policy Brief, Issue 10. Retrieved February 21, 2008, from http://www.communityinclusion.org/article.php?article_id=21&staff_id=36&style=print

Stoddard, S. & Kraus, L. (2006). Arranging for personal assistance services and assistive technology at work. A report of the Rehabilitation Research and Training Center on Personal Assistance Services. Disability and Rehabilitation: Assistive Technology, 1 (1-2), 89-95.

Ticket to Work and Work Incentives Improvement Act of 1999, 42 U.S.C §1320b-22(b)(2)(B)(ii) (2009).

Turner, E. (2007, August). Personal Assistance Services. PAS Facts, 1, Retrieved February 28, 2008, from http://www.worksupport.com/documents/PASFACTSVol1.pdf ["Turner1 (2007)"]

Turner, E. (2007, August). Finding a Workplace Personal Assistant. PAS Facts, 2, Retrieved February 28, 2008, from http://www.worksupport.com/documents/PASFACTSVol2.pdf ["Turner2 (2007)"]

U.S. Department of Labor, Office of Disability Employment Policy. (2006, August). Personal Assistance Services (WPAS) in the Workplace. Job Accommodation Network (JAN) Accommodation and Compliance Series, Retrieved March 3, 2008, from http://www.jan.wvu.edu/media/PAS.html

INDEX OF FORMS AND WORKSHEETS

TRANSITIONING TO LIVING INDEPENDENTLY

IDENTIFYING WHAT YOU'RE LOOKING FOR IN A PERSONAL ASSISTANT

SEARCHING FOR PAS

MANAGING A PERSONAL ASSISTANT